NOAH'S BIG BOAT

This story has been extracted from
Read Aloud Bible Stories, Vol. 3
by Ella Lindvall

Printed in Mexico

MOODY PRESS

Noah was God's friend.
Noah made God happy.
Noah tried to do
just what God told him.

Now Noah had three boys.
Their names were Shem
and Ham and Japheth.

God said, "Noah,
make a big houseboat.
Water is coming.
Water will cover up
everything.
You will be safe on the boat."
And Noah did what God told him.

God said, "Make rooms
in the boat."
Noah made rooms.
God said, "Make a window
in the boat."
Noah made a window.
God said, "Make a door
in the boat."
Noah made a door.

God said, "Put something
to eat
on the boat."
Noah did
what God told him.
God said,
"Put animals
on the boat."
Noah did
what God told him.
Into the houseboat went—

Mr. and Mrs. Cat,
Mr. and Mrs. Horse,
Mr. and Mrs. Dog,
Mr. and Mrs. Pig,
Mr. and Mrs. Grasshopper,
Mr. and Mrs. Wooly Worm,
Mr. and Mrs. Duck,
and more animals too.
Then God said,

"Now you and your family
get on the boat."
So Mr. and Mrs. Noah
got on the boat.
Mr. and Mrs. Shem
got on the boat.
Mr. and Mrs. Ham
got on the boat.
Mr. and Mrs. Japheth
got on the boat.
And THEN

God shut the door.
After a while,
down came the rain,
DRIP, DRIP, DRIP.
After a while,
up came the water,
SPLASH, SPLASH, SPLASH.
Soon—

water ran over the streets.
Water ran over the houses.
Water ran over the little hills.
Water ran over the big hills.

Now the houseboat was floating!
But Noah was safe inside.
His family was safe inside.
The animals were safe inside.

Noah's family
had something to eat.
They gave the animals
something to eat.
Then they waited.
They waited till the water
went away.
They waited till God said,
"IT'S TIME TO GET OFF
THE BOAT."

Noah did
what God told him.
Mr. and Mrs. Noah
got off the boat.
Mr. and Mrs. Shem
got off the boat.
Mr. and Mrs. Ham
got off the boat.
Mr. and Mrs. Japheth
got off the boat.

All the animals
got off the boat.
They walked and ran
and crawled and hopped.
God said,

"Don't worry.
The water won't come back.
The water won't cover up
the world anymore."
(It never has.)
And God made a rainbow.

What did you learn?

Noah did just what God said.
God took care of Noah.
God takes care
of all the mommies and daddies
and boys and girls
who do what He says.
You too.

About the Author

Ella K. Lindvall (A.B., Taylor University; Wheaton College; Northern Illinois University) is a mother and former elementary school teacher. She is the author of *The Bible Illustrated for Little Children,* and *Read-Aloud Bible Stories, volumes I, II, and III.*